# The Wicked Will Not Go Unpunished

## Dr Daniel Olukoya

# THE WICKED WILL NOT GO UNPUNISHED

© 2013. Dr Daniel Olukoya

**A publication of**
**MOUNTAIN OF FIRE AND MIRACLES MINISTRIES**
13, Olasimbo Street, off Olumo Road, Onike,
P. O. Box 2990, Sabo, Yaba, Lagos, Nigeria.

ISBN: 978-978-920-077-1

For further information or permission contact:
Email: pasteurdanielolukoya_french@yahoo.fr
mfmhqworldwide@mountainoffire.org

Or visit our website: www.mountainoffire.org
http://mfmbiligualbooks4evangelism.blogspot.com/

The title of our message is, "the wicked will not go unpunished" I would like you to read it very carefully because it addresses the root of man's problems and the reason why many people are going through one ordeal or another.

Proverbs 11:21 says,
*"Though hand join in hand, the wicked shall not be unpunished: but the seed of the righteous shall be delivered."*

Though hand join in hand means no matter how tight the cooperation may be, no matter how smart they are, no matter how cleverly they are concealed, no matter the walls they have built, no matter their technique of hiding, no matter the kind of meeting they have held, no matter the agreement between them, the wicked shall not go unpunished.

When sin is the driver, you can be 100 per cent sure that shame is at the back seat. The worst enemy of man is his sinful heart propelled and fueled by Mr. Flesh.

Sometimes, sin hooks a man in the process of trying to obtain something he does not have, when he is afraid that he may lose something he already has. I want you to understand that there is no small sin. When you come to the service and disturb others from concentrating, you are a sinner. There is no small sin. The consequences of what you may consider as a small sin may be immeasurable. If you are sinning because you want to make some profit, you are wasting time because you cannot profit by sin, it is impossible. Anything you gain from sin would be taken back from you by sin. And you would pay back with interest. Sin is like a small child playing with a snake, the child may find the snake very beautiful and interesting. But the snake only remains interesting as long as it has not done its worse. Everyone has power to choose his or her sins but nobody has power to choose the consequences of those sins. Every sin has a consequence and punishment assigned to it. So, once you commit a sin, punishment is automatic. And when sin enters, it will cause the cup of joy to leak. Therefore, as soon as the seed of sin is sowed, judgment is sure. Unfortunately, the Bible says, "…One sinner destroyeth much good" (Ecclesiastes 9:18). The sin of one person can bring tragedy to many. Everybody in the boat of Jonah would have been killed because the Lord was not ready to negotiate with him at all. Perhaps you are the Jonah in your family. That is you are the reason why waves and storms are blowing across your family. Perhaps God has brought you up to do something there which you have neglected and since you are not doing the will of God, the evil and mad wind of life is blowing against your family. People make a mistake by thinking that sin is judged the way it appears. Sin is not judged the way you see it, but the way God sees it. And when God wants to start His judgment, where He would start may be very strange to you. For example, when God wants to judge the sin of an armed robber, He would not start and end with the armed robber alone. He could begin His judgment with the mother of the armed robber who was a fornicator or an adulterer. From there, He could move to the person who was selling him Marijuana and from there to the woman who had the bar where he was drinking pepper soup and alcohol and from there to the person who introduced him to robbery. So, God packs so many people together when He begins to judge a sinner. He will not judge according to your opinion. You may say, "In my own opinion, I don't think what I have done is that bad, after all everybody is doing it." You may be very wrong because you might have caused more harm than anyone else who did it.

The repercussions of the same sin committed by two or more different people may be completely different. For example, if God ordains a sister to be a prophetess and decrees that through her shall be a seed that shall save Africa. And that sister commits only one abortion to remove that seed, the repercussion of her sin would be greater than some women who will do twenty abortions because their seeds would have been for a different purpose.

Prices of materials may rise and fall but the wages of sin remain the same. The Bible says, "The wages of sin is death." (Romans 6:23). The most expensive thing in the world is sin because for the purpose of sin, God allowed His own Son to be killed. Many people are now becoming new sinners. There are new sinners every day; academic sinners, intellectual sinners, brainy sinners, psychological sinners, etc. But there is no new sin. Sin is still the same.

Beloved, I want you to understand that wickedness never goes unpunished. Though hand join in hand, no sinner shall go unpunished. The pleasure of sin is paid with sorrow. And any sin you cover up will eventually bring you down because sin is the greatest of all detectives. The Bible says, "Be sure that your sin will find you out"(Numbers 32:23). A certain man strangulated a young girl after raping her. He dragged her body to a bush path and walked home. His wife noticed that his coat was a bit rough and that he had lost one button. Innocently, she told him that one button was missing from his coat and demanded to know what happened. He knew surely well that the button must be at the site where he killed the girl. So, he lost his peace. Policemen arrived at the site of the murder, saw the girl's body and began to look for clues around. Only one of them found the button and hid it in his pocket. It was not in the newspapers that a button was found at the site of the murder. But the man still had no peace. Something kept reminding him of the button. He became very restless. Two months later, he decided to go to the site to look for the button. Immediately, he arrived there looking at the ground, the police arrested him. They said, "We know what you are looking for. You are looking for your button." And he said, "Yes." His sin eventually found him out. The Bible says, "Your sin shall find you out." It is the greatest detective. The children you had outside wedlock, which you are hiding from your legally married spouse will grow and eventually come back and destroy the family. Your sin will find you out. Every sin, no matter how little has consequences. Even the misuse of the tongue has consequences. You must understand this very well.

Number 12:1 says,
*"And Miriam and Aaron spake against Moses because of the Ethiopian woman whom he had married; for he had married an Ethiopian woman."*

They just spoke against Moses, they did not fight him and something happened. Numbers 12:9-14 says,

*"And the anger of the Lord was kindled against them; and he departed. And the cloud departed from off the tabernacle; and, behold, Miriam became leprous, white as snow: and Aaron looked upon Miriam and, behold she was leprous. And Aaron said unto Moses, Alas, my lord, I beseech thee, lay not the sin upon us, wherein we have done foolishly, and wherein we have sinned. Let her not be as one dead, of whom the flesh is half consumed when he cometh out of his mother's womb. And Moses cried unto the Lord, saying, Heal her now, O God, I beseech thee. And the Lord said unto Moses, If her father had but spit in her face, should she not be ashamed seven days? Let her be shut out from the camp seven days, and after that let her be received in again."*

It was this Miriam that put Moses in the river, when he was a baby. She was also the person that called the attention of the daughter of Pharaoh to Moses. Numbers 12:15 says, "And Miriam was shut out from the camp seven days; and the people journeyed not till Miriam was brought in again." God disciplined Miriam and Moses cried, "Heal her now O Lord." God said, "Yes, I can forgive but forgiveness does not eliminate discipline." God dealt with her for seven days. She would have died but the Lord just had mercy.

2 Samuel chapter 12 tells us a story about David. One day, David, instead of going to battle, was lazing about. Eventually, he saw Bathsheba, another man's wife, having a bath. He took her and killed her husband. And the Prophet of God came unto David.

2 Samuel 12:7 – 16 says, "And Nathan said to David, Thou art the man. Thus saith the Lord God of Israel, I anointed thee king over Israel, and I delivered thee out of the hand of Saul; And I gave thee thy master's house, and thy master's wives into thy bosom, and gave thee the house of Israel and of Judah; and if that had been too little, I would moreover have given unto thee such and such things. Wherefore hast thou despised the commandment of the Lord, to do evil in his sight? Thou hast killed Uriah the Hittite with the sword, and hast taken his wife to be thy wife, and hast slain him with the sword of the children of Ammon, Now therefore, (No.1) the sword shall never depart from thine house; because thou hast despised me, and hast taken the wife of Uriah the Hittite to be thy wife. (No2) Behold I will raise up evil against thee out of thine own house, (No3) I

will take thy wives before thine eyes, and give them unto thy neighbour; and he shall lie with thy wives in the sight of this sun. For thou didst it secretly: but I will do this thing before all Israel, and before the sun. And David said unto Nathan, I have sinned against the Lord. And Nathan said unto David, The Lord also hath put away thy sin; thou shalt not die. Howbeit, because by this deed thou hast given great occasion to the enemies of the Lord to blaspheme, the child also that is born unto thee shall surely die. And Nathan departed unto his house. And the Lord struck the child that Uriah's wife bare unto David, and it was very sick. David therefore besought God for the child; and David fasted, and went in, and lay all night upon the earth." But the child still died. God forgave David his sin. The forgiveness removed the condemnation and the sin in the record of God. But it did not eliminate the discipline. It did not remove the consequences. Thou hand join in hand, no sinner shall go unpunished.

A person who commits adultery, and after contacting HIV begins to call upon God to forgive and heal him would be forgiven and will make heaven. But the consequences of his sin which is HIV will still punish and kill him.

Sometime ago, at a pastors' conference, there was an argument between two pastors. One of them was so annoyed that he said he would drop the Bible and deal with the other one. After the conference, the vehicle he boarded was involved in a nasty accident and everybody in that vehicle except him walked out without any scratch. He broke his two legs.

At the Orthopaedic hospital where he was admitted, he asked the Lord why that had to happen to him and the Lord said, "You said you would drop the Bible and you did. You really dropped it." The pastor said, "But I have asked you to forgive me." And God said, "Yes if not you would have died. The Bible has been your support and shade and you said you will drop it." He still has a bad leg today as a testimony to the discipline that he received.

God has facility to forgive every sin but no one can tell the extent of the consequences. There is nothing anyone can do about it. The consequence will take its toll. According to the book of Revelation, after you have read through the whole of the Bible and decide to continue to do evil, you are free to do so. But it says, "Behold, I come quickly and my reward is with me." Samson's hair grew again but his eyes never got opened. Abraham brought forth Ishmael, and the consequences are clearly seen now. God may forgive sin but it will have consequences. Unfortunately, some of these consequences may remain with a person throughout his life. So, every sin you are living in today is a foundation for your generation. The sins will find you out and find out members of your generation. That is why we have to be very careful. If Gehazi had known that collecting money from Naaman would affect his offspring, he would not have done it. Through his action he planted an evil seed for his generation.

Every sin you commit will find you out. You cannot be cleverer than sin. It will eventually find you out. When you ask God to forgive you, He will and you will make heaven. But the forgiveness sometimes does not free you from the consequences of your actions. There are some wrongs you may do which could be redressed. For example, if you steal somebody's money, and you repent and make restitution by returning the money, your punishment will be limited because the wrong has already been corrected. But there are some sins that cannot be right; forgiveness does not free one from accountability. David committed the sin of sexual immorality, deception and murder, and when the consequences started, under the banner of sexual immorality; his own son raped his own daughter. His own son Absalom was sleeping with his wives on the roof top. David practised deception. His son Absalom too deceived him. David killed only Uriah but he lost three children. He lost the baby that resulted from the adultery, Amnon and Absalom. These were the consequences. So, if you do not want your children to become robbers, do not train them with stolen money. If you do not want your children to have broken home, do not beat up your spouse before them. If you do not want your children to go into drugs, do not get involved in drug business yourself. If you do not want somebody to mess up your own daughter, do not mess up somebody else's daughter.

## MERCY OF GOD

Sometimes, when people commit sin, they would say, "Blood of Jesus." The blood of Jesus does not eliminate the consequences of sin. It would only remove the condemnation. The only thing that can eliminate the consequences of sin is the mercy of God.

The trouble with the mercy of God is that it is not guaranteed. The Bible says, "I will have mercy on whom I will have mercy" (Romans 9:15). That is, that mercy is not guaranteed. You may ask God to have mercy on you, and He would say, "Not today."

Beloved, I would like you to know that sin is success in nothing. It is self-inflicted nonsense. It invites death. Sin obscures the soul. Sin can sometimes come as a friend, but the longer you stay in sin, the less and less it bothers you. Then you become hardened if you do not quickly run out of it. If you take a frog and throw it into boiling water, it will jump out. But if you put a frog in a kettle of cold water and put the kettle on fire and begin to warn it little by little, the frog will not jump out. It will be enjoying the warmth of the water until it is boiled to death.

That is what sin does. Only one leak in a ship is enough to sink the whole ship. One sin can destroy a person totally. Do not compare yourself to other people. Your life is different likewise your destiny. So, do not copy others. Do not follow a multitude to commit sin. One little sin can cause great trouble. The sin you consider small and light could send you to the tail of destiny. We need the mercy of God. We need to cry to Him for mercy. Mercy is obtained in the prison of discipline. If you want to obtain mercy today, tell God the truth. If you tell Him the truth, you stand a better chance of receiving mercy. Though hand join in hand, no sinner will go unpunished.

Many people need to sort out themselves with the Lord. Why should you repeat the errors that have killed many people?

The Bible says, "These things were written for our learning that through the comfort of the scriptures we might have hope. Keeping evil friends, drinking, smoking, inordinate affection, unholy relationship, lying, malice, grudges, pride etc have their consequences. To open your mouth and say that you are tired of prayer has its own consequences. Rumour mongering, gossiping, slander and all forms of misuse of the mouth have their consequences. There are consequences also for allowing your talent to lie fallow. The man with one talent in the Bible did not commit murder. He did not commit fornication neither did he rape anybody. His offence was that he did not use his talent. He buried it and because of that he went to hell fire. There is a consequence for running away from the agenda of God for your life. Trying to pay somebody back in his own coin has its consequences.

It would be a sad thing if you appear at the gate of life, and your name appears on the book of the house fellowship and the register of your church but it is not found in the Book of life. The Bible says, "One book shall be opened and other books too shall be opened, and then another book shall be opened which is the book of life. If your name is found in all those other books and because of one little sin, it is not found in the Book of life, what do you do? Do not end up living a wasted life. You should cry to the Lord from the bottom of your heart for His mercy. The Bible says, "Though hand join in hand, no sinner shall go unpunished." It did not say no sinner shall go unforgiven.

## PRAYER POINTS

1. My Father, have mercy on me today, in the name of Jesus.

2. Blood of Jesus, clear away every sin that wants to destroy my destiny, in the name of Jesus.

3. Personal spiritual chains, ancestral chains, break, in the name of Jesus.

4. Every ancient prison door in my family line, break, in the name of Jesus.

5. Every gap between where I am and where God wants me to be, close by fire, in the name of Jesus.

*Thank you Jesus!!!*

# MFM praise and worship songs

Let God arise,
Let His enemies be scattered; (*let poverty, problems,
sickness etc be scattered*) x3
Let God  x2
Arise
Alleluia
*****************************************

Evil plantations
Come out now in
Jesus name.
Come out !!!
*****************************************

If I be a child of God, let fire fall.
*****************************************

Arise oh God Arise x2
And fight my battles!
Arise oh Lord Arise x2
*****************************************

Elohim x2
Jehovah! You are God
Elohim x2
Jehovah! You are God
*****************************************

Immortal God, Invisible God, Immortal God, how great thou art !
*****************************************

Verily x2
You are good
Jesus you are good
*****************************************

You are Alpha and Omega, We worship you our God, you are worthy to be praised!
*****************************************

Unquestionably you are the Lord!  X2
Unquestionably x2
Unquestionably you are the Lord!
*****************************************

I can see everything turning around for my favour !
*****************************************

He is a miracle working God x2
He is Alpha and Omega
He is a miracle working God

# [ ABOUT D. K. OLUKOYA ]

Dr. D. K. Olukoya is the General Overseer of the Mountain of Fire and Miracles Ministries and the Battle Cry Ministries. He holds a First Class Honours Degree in Microbiology from the University of Lagos, Nigeria and a Ph.D. in Molecular Genetics from the University of Reading, United Kingdom. As a researcher, he has over eighty scientific publications to his credit. Anointed by God, Dr. Olukoya is a teacher, prophet, evangelist and preacher of the word. His life and that of his wife, Shade and their son, Elijah Toluwani, are living proofs that all power belongs to God.

## ABOUT MOUNTAIN OF FIRE AND MIRACLES MINISTRIES

Mountain of Fire and Miracles Ministries, is a ministry devoted to the revival of apostolic signs, Holy Ghost fireworks and the unlimited demonstration of the power of God to deliver to the uttermost. Absolute holiness within and without, as the greatest spiritual insecticide, and a condition for heaven is taught openly. MFM is a do-it-yourself Gospel Ministry, where your hands are trained to wage war and your fingers to fight.

A brief history of Mountain of Fire and Miracles Ministries Incorporated
The Mountain of Fire and Miracles was founded in 1989. The first meeting was held at the home of Dr. D. K Olukoya and had

24 persons in attendance. The Church later moved to No. 60, Old Yaba Road, Lagos, and then to the present International Headquarters, site on 24th April, 1994. The Mountain of Fire and Miracles Ministries' Headquarters is the largest single Christian congregation in Africa, with attendance of over 200,000 in single meetings. Mountain of Fire and Miracles Ministries is a full gospel ministry devoted to the revival of apostolic signs, Holy Ghost fireworks and the unlimited demonstration of the power of God to deliver to the uttermost. Absolute holiness, within and without, as the greatest spiritual insecticide and a pre-requisite for heaven is taught openly. MFM is a do-it-yourself Gospel ministry, where your hands are trained to wage war and your fingers to do battle.

www.ingramcontent.com/pod-product-compliance
Lightning Source LLC
Chambersburg PA
CBHW060605030426
42337CB00019B/3613